DEAD OR ALIVE?

Clive Gifford
Illustrated by Sarah Horne

Consultancy by David Burnie

RED SHED

EGMONT

Contents

Introduction

Every day, millions of creatures are locked in a battle for survival . . .

Many living things on land, in the sea and in the air have to tackle the tough environment they dwell in – where lack of food and water or extreme temperatures can threaten their existence.

Other living things are constantly looking over their shoulder, if they have one, in fear of attack. Many creatures are always just one wrong move away from ending up as lunch or dinner for other hungry critters. Some are forced to fake death to avoid the real thing, whilst others sacrifice themselves so that members of their group or colony are not killed.

This book will guide you through the extraordinary ways nature has equipped some creatures to survive, and how they live and die. So, if you want to learn all about some seriously long-living things, creatures that laugh in the face of impending doom, heart-warming tales of heroism, and how some unfortunate animals lose their minds and become zombies, then you've come to the right place.

Some animals are real frauds and fakers. They pretend to be dead as a way of staying alive. Sounds nuts, but it's true. You see, many animals who hunt others – predators – are fussy eaters. To avoid getting ill from eating rotting meat, they will only eat animals they kill themselves.

So, a brilliant way to outwit a nasty meat-eater is to fake your own death before it attacks you, especially if you cannot outmuscle or outrun the fierce animal hunting you down.

Today's Specials

Beetle Bites

Many spiders only track moving prey, so some species of beetle, such as the red flour beetle, have learned to stay stock-still. They pretend to be dead so the spider will move on to capture and scoff another beetle, or other insect, that is foolishly on the move.

Opossum Snacks

Opossums are found in North America. When under threat, opossums go into a state of shock. They fall on to their side, go rigid and thick drool develops round their snout. They won't move or react even if turned, prodded or dragged. They stay in this state for between 40 minutes and four hours. Scientists call this tonic immobility.

DROOL DRIPS OUT OF THE MOUTH

BUBBLES COME OUT OF THE NOSE

LEGS GO RIGID AND STICK STRAIGHT OUT

BAD SMELL IS RELEASED BY GLANDS IN THE BOTTOM

EYES CLOSE OR HALF CLOSE

Animal Oscars

When it comes to playing dead, the award-winning animal actor has to be the hognose snake. When threatened, it can put on a convincing display of death. The reason the hognose deserves to win an Oscar is because it can choose whether it acts dead or not, unlike the opossum and other creatures, which have no control over their acting ability.

Plan A: Snake's Alive

When threatened, the hognose snake's first bit of acting sees it flatten out its head to look more fierce and deadly. Sometimes, this is enough to ward off predators, which are fearful of being bitten by an aggressive snake.

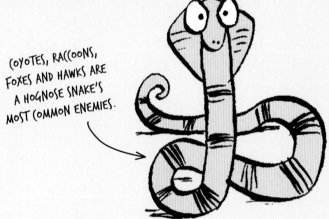

COYOTES, RACCOONS, FOXES AND HAWKS ARE A HOGNOSE SNAKE'S MOST COMMON ENEMIES.

Plan B: Stinky Stuff

If plan A doesn't work, the hognose moves to plan B – playing dead. BUT THERE'S MORE! The sly snake gives off a disgusting, rotting smell and sometimes lets some of its droppings ooze out of its body. Urgh! If this has put you off your next meal, imagine being the creature that was going to snack on it!

THE SNAKE'S STAR PERFORMANCE PUTS OFF ITS PREDATORS.

OPOSSUM

I can't believe that I didn't win.

COYOTE

That sneaky snake was too smelly for me to eat. Grrrrr!

Attack!

Creatures don't play dead just to stop predators taking a bite out of them. Some predators are sneaky and feign death or illness to lure another animal close enough to them so that *they* can attack.

LIVINGSTONE'S CICHLID

Oh look, a free lunch . . . yummy!

My thoughts precisely!

Dead Hungry

The Livingstone's cichlid is a fish found in east African lakes. When it's feeling peckish, the fish will keel over on its side and its skin goes blotchier than usual. To other fish, it looks like a goner. When fish that feed off dead fish – scavengers – swim over to take a nibble, the Livingstone's cichlid grabs one and gobbles it up. They don't chase meals, meals come to them!

Excellent – here comes dinner!

Bad Vibrations

Spiders spin webs to trap insects in their sticky strands. However, assassin bugs are ingenious insects that turn the tables on spiders. Using its legs, an assassin bug carefully plucks the strands of a spider's web. This causes the web to vibrate as if an insect is struggling to escape.

The spider senses these vibrations and heads over thinking it's time for lunch. It is lunchtime . . . but only for the assassin bug! The bug stabs the spider with its beak to kill it and then scoffs it.

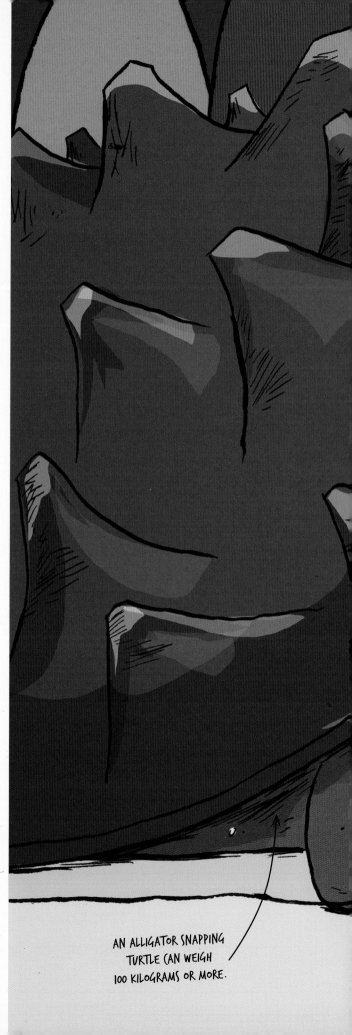

AN ALLIGATOR SNAPPING TURTLE CAN WEIGH 100 KILOGRAMS OR MORE.

Cave Grave

Playing dead or pretending to be in trouble is not the only way to get lunch. Some creatures simply lie motionless and pretend to be something else. The deadly alligator snapping turtle pretends to be a rock. These North American turtles lie completely still in the water with their giant jaws wide open. Their grey colour makes them look like a small cave.

Stop! I don't think this is a cave at all . . . Gulp!

THE TURTLE'S TONGUE LOOKS LIKE A WORM. FISH, FROGS AND OTHER RIVER CREATURES ARE ATTRACTED TO THE 'WORM', BUT THEN GET A SHARP SURPRISE AS THE TURTLE'S JAWS SNAP SHUT WITH FEARSOME FORCE. CRUNCH!

THIS IS WHAT AN ALLIGATOR SNAPPING TURTLE ACTUALLY LOOKS LIKE!

CAVE THIS WAY

Dead in Days

Whilst many creatures are battling for survival, there are others that don't hang around long enough to worry too much about being gobbled up. Wild cottontail rabbits tend to munch away on grass and carrots for just three years, whilst the tiny pygmy shrew lives for only a third of that time at most. Here are some creatures that exist for even less time.

PARP!

4 MONTHS OLD TODAY

I'm three days old, you know.

Hairy Backs

Hairy backs is the nickname given to tiny creatures called gastrotrichs. They live in the spaces between grains of sand and mud, or on aquatic plants. Many are smaller than the full stop at the end of this sentence.

Freshwater gastrotrichs go from eggs to adults in three days and then die. In laboratories some may last a week or slightly longer, but many perish before then.

Growing Up Together

Labord's chameleons are found only on the Indian Ocean island of Madagascar. They all hatch from eggs in November. After about eight months inside their egg, they have to be busy little creatures when they come out – because they have just four months to grow into adults, find a mate and create the next generation of Labord's chameleons.

A Long Wait

Dragonflies are some of the most patient creatures. There are more than 5,000 species of dragonfly, and some species of these winged insects can remain as larvae for up to five years. Once they finally emerge as adult dragonflies, they live for between a few weeks and five months.

GIANT SOUTHERN DARNER DRAGONFLIES ARE FAST FLIERS. THEY CAN ZIP ALONG AT SPEEDS OF OVER 60 KILOMETRES PER HOUR.

LABORD'S CHAMELEONS ARE MOSTLY GREEN BUT FEMALES DISPLAY DAZZLING ORANGE, RED AND YELLOW COLOURS ON THEIR BODIES TO ATTRACT MATES.

A MAYFLY'S MOUTH PARTS ARE JUST FOR SHOW. THEY DON'T LIVE LONG ENOUGH TO GET HUNGRY!

Cheers!

Time Flies

The 'blink and you'll miss it' award goes to the adult mayfly. These winged insects hatch from eggs into nymphs that live under water. They can stay as nymphs for many months but when they turn into adults, the clock really starts ticking. Adult mayflies only live for a day, some for less than that.

Long-living Legends

In 1997, Jeanne Louise Calment celebrated her 122nd birthday, making her the oldest-known human being. But some creatures live even longer. Check out these old-timers.

Having a Whale of a Time

The biggest of our long-living stars is the bowhead whale. Living in the chilly waters of the northern parts of our planet, the males can reach 18 metres long and weigh up to 100 tonnes. Bowheads can live for up to 210 years. Harpoon tips that are 150 years old have been found embedded in the skin of some bowheads!

Jeanne, you're a spring chicken – I am over 200 years old!

A BOWHEAD WHALE HAS TWO BLOWHOLES THROUGH WHICH IT CAN SPURT WATER UP TO SEVEN METRES HIGH.

Travelling Tortoise

Many species of giant tortoise live to a ripe old age. Harriet, a Galapagos tortoise, was collected by scientist Charles Darwin in 1835 and sailed with him back to England. Harriet was then taken to Australia in 1842, where she lived until she was 175.

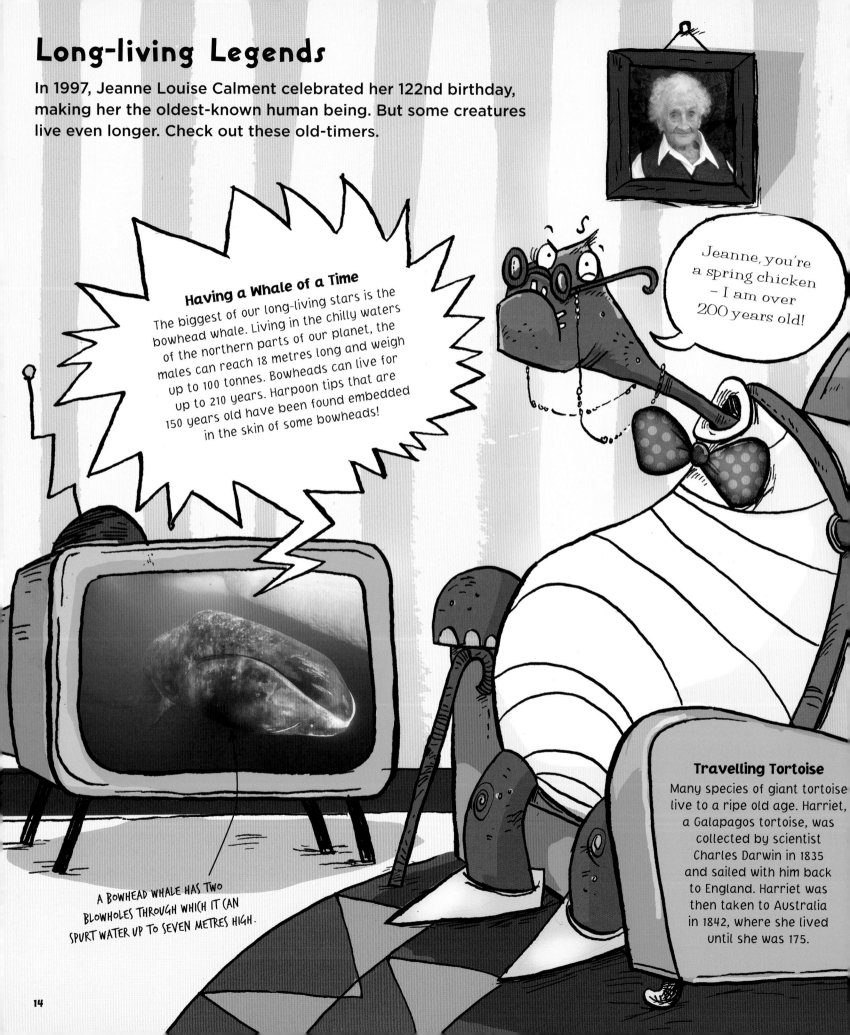

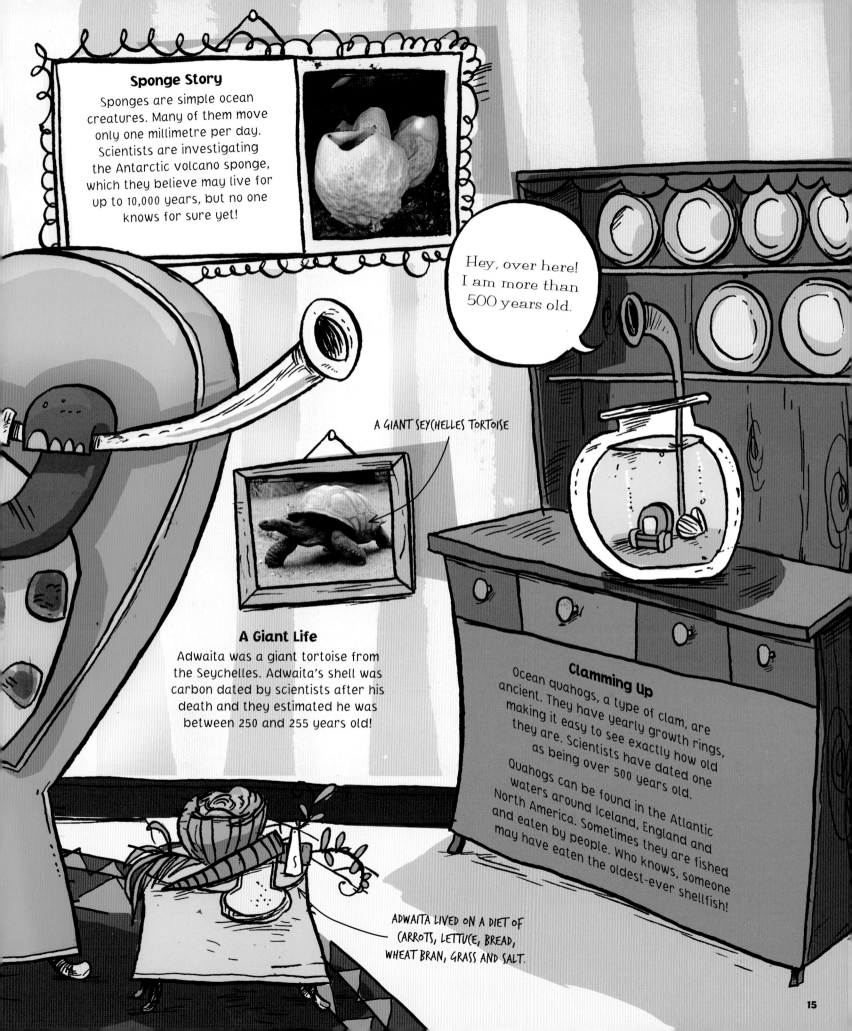

Sponge Story

Sponges are simple ocean creatures. Many of them move only one millimetre per day. Scientists are investigating the Antarctic volcano sponge, which they believe may live for up to 10,000 years, but no one knows for sure yet!

Hey, over here! I am more than 500 years old.

A GIANT SEYCHELLES TORTOISE

A Giant Life

Adwaita was a giant tortoise from the Seychelles. Adwaita's shell was carbon dated by scientists after his death and they estimated he was between 250 and 255 years old!

Clamming Up

Ocean quahogs, a type of clam, are ancient. They have yearly growth rings, making it easy to see exactly how old they are. Scientists have dated one as being over 500 years old.

Quahogs can be found in the Atlantic waters around Iceland, England and North America. Sometimes they are fished and eaten by people. Who knows, someone may have eaten the oldest-ever shellfish!

ADWAITA LIVED ON A DIET OF CARROTS, LETTUCE, BREAD, WHEAT BRAN, GRASS AND SALT.

Pigeon Power

Homing pigeons are amazing navigators, able to fly hundreds of kilometres back to their homes without a satnav or maps. For centuries they provided the first airmail letters; people took pigeons with them on journeys and then tied a written message to them – usually round their leg – before letting them fly home.

Aerial Espionage

During World War I, armies used thousands of homing pigeons. Most became messengers, taking reports from the front line back to headquarters, but some were used as spy photographers. Each spy was fitted with an automatic camera that snapped photos as the bird flew over battlefields.

Sergeant Stubby: Dog Hero

Stubby, an American bull terrier, spent 18 months in the trenches with US troops during World War I. He saved many lives by alerting soldiers to poisonous gas attacks and tracking down the wounded.

Promoted to 'Sergeant' for his bravery, Stubby was injured twice; once in a grenade explosion and once by poisonous gas. Both times he was given five-star hospital treatment. After the war ended he was awarded a number of medals and met two US presidents.

Not Dead Yet Pets

Pets are amazing, but some are more incredible than others – capable of surviving life-threatening events to be reunited with their loving owners. Ahhhh!

A purrfect landing!

Canine Castaway

Sophie Tucker, an Australian cattle dog, was believed to have drowned when storm waves washed her off her owners' boat in the Pacific Ocean. Yet, four months later, her owners were astonished to be reunited with their precious pooch.

It turned out that brave Sophie had doggy-paddled her way through eight kilometres of shark-infested waters to reach a remote little island, called St Bees, off the coast of Australia. She had managed to live on the deserted island before being recovered by park rangers.

Nineteen-floor Feline

Life remains sweet for Sugar the cat, even though she survived a big fall in 2012. We're not talking about tumbling off a garden fence; Sugar fell from the window of a 19-floor flat in Boston, USA, and hit the ground 60 metres below. OUCH!

Amazingly, Sugar jumped up and trotted back into the building – she had suffered no broken bones or big injuries. Sugar didn't get so close to windows again for a while, though!

He's gone!

Gasp!

Lady in a Lifeboat

When *HMS Titanic* sank in the Atlantic Ocean in 1912, thousands of humans and nine dogs perished, but one little Pomeranian, called Lady, survived. Her owner, Margaret Hays, wrapped her up in a blanket and bundled her into one of the lifeboats.

I'm Rhino, the amazing hamster escape artist!

Dead and Buried

Poor Rhino the hamster looked dead. He was stiff and not breathing when his sad owner, David Eyley, went to work one morning. That evening, he placed the stiff hamster in a plastic container and buried him in a 70-centimetre deep hole in his back garden in Wantage, England.

Whilst at work the next day, though, David received a phone call from his neighbour and rushed home to find Rhino running around his neighbour's garden. The heroic hamster had come round, muscled his way out of the coffin and burrowed his way upwards and out of the hole.

DEATH-DEFYING DAILY

DEATH-DEFYING TWO TWO SAVE THEIR BACON

Some animals have looked death in the eye, given it a cheeky little wink and then carried on living. Meet some of the animals that have genuinely cheated sure-fire death through ingenuity and bravery.

TAMWORTH TWO TWO SAVE THEIR BACON

Two five-month-old Tamworth breed pigs didn't like the look of their fate as a truck carried them to an abattoir in Wiltshire, England, in order to turn them into meat for the butcher.

So, soon after arriving at the abattoir, they escaped! They squeezed their way through a gap in a fence and then swam across the River Avon.

The pigs went on the run and attracted lots of media attention. News reporters flocked to the area and nicknamed the pair the Tamworth Two. The porkers eluded capture for more than a week.

AN HOUR-LONG TV SHOW WAS MADE IN THE UK ABOUT THE PIGS.

ONE IN THE STY FOR THE BUTCHER, AS THE PIGS – NICKNAMED BUTCH AND SUNDANCE – SWAM FOR THEIR LIVES.

When they were finally caught, it wasn't off to the butcher but to an animal conservation centre in Kent to live happy, long lives. A newspaper company had bought the pair of plucky pigs to save their bacon!

PEG-LEG PONY

When Hurricane Katrina struck the coast of the United States in 2005, many people upped and fled, abandoning pets and other animals they owned. Molly the pony was one such animal. She survived the hurricane and lived on her own for several weeks before she was rescued and taken to an animal sanctuary.

That's a strange, swirly neigh-bour coming my way.

However, whilst at the sanctuary, Molly was attacked by a pit bull terrier who bit her legs, one of which got infected and had to be cut off. That would normally mean the end for a horse, as it would be put down, but a kind surgeon made a prosthetic (artificial) leg complete with a hoof for Molly to wear, so she could live a happy life.

Yee-haa!

FLUSHED WITH SUCCESS

Things looked grim for a cocker spaniel puppy when four-year-old Daniel Blair accidentally flushed him down the toilet in England. The puppy travelled round the u-bend and down the stinky sewage pipes, where he was trapped in a pipe deep underground beneath another house.

A drains company was called out and located the puppy using tiny cameras. After almost four hours, the puppy was pulled out of a manhole . . . alive! The puppy was named Dyno in honour of the company who saved him.

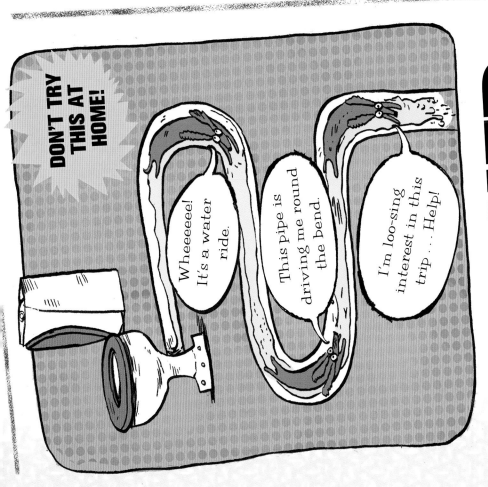

DON'T TRY THIS AT HOME!

Wheeeee! It's a water ride.

This pipe is driving me round the bend.

I'm loo-sing interest in this trip . . . Help!

Extinct?

All sorts of creatures, from the smallest bacteria to giant dinosaurs, such as Tyrannosaurus rex, have died out – never to return. Scientists call this extinction. However, some creatures that were once thought to be extinct, have surprised scientists by turning up very much alive and kicking.

Hey! Get me down, I don't belong here!

THE LORD HOWE ISLAND STICK INSECT IS A WHOPPER. IT CAN GROW UP TO 15 CENTIMETRES LONG AND IS NICKNAMED A 'WALKING SAUSAGE' DUE TO ITS STOUT BODY.

LORD HOWE ISLAND STICK INSECT

Sticky Situation

The Lord Howe Island stick insect was declared extinct in 1930, but 71 years later, a group of fewer than 30 of these creatures was found living underneath a bush on a tiny, nearby rock called Ball's Pyramid in the Pacific Ocean.

Only joking! I'm still alive, you know!

Who are you calling a sausage?

Watch the Birdie

The takahé is a flightle bird. In 1848 it was declared extinct but then in the 20th century, a handful of birds were found in an isolated valley in New Zealand. An estimated 225 birds now live there.

Chalet Creature
The mountain pygmy possum was believed to have died out thousands of years ago. But, in 1966, one was discovered nibbling berries in an Australian ski chalet. Now, around 2,000 are thought to exist.

EXTINCT EXHIBITS

THE MOUNTAIN PYGMY POSSUM WEIGHS ABOUT 45 GRAMS — THAT'S LESS THAN A CHICKEN EGG!

LA PALMA GIANT LIZARD

Derek, stop pretending to be extinct!

Lizards Alive
In 2007, Luis Minguez was hiking in the Canary Islands when he photographed a 30-centimetre-long lizard. It turned out to be La Palma giant lizard – a creature thought to have died out in 1500.

COELACANTHS CAN GROW UP TO 1.8 METRES LONG. THAT'S LONGER THAN THE AVERAGE ADULT MALE HUMAN.

COELACANTH

Dino Fish
In 1938, Captain Hendrick Goosen caught an unusual fish off the coast of South Africa. It was a fish he'd never seen before, but with good reason; the coelacanth was a species that was thought to have been extinct for over 65 million years!

A second specimen was caught in 1952 and since then a few dozen examples of this dino fish have been found in the waters off the coast of east Africa.

Hibernation

Have you ever woken up on a bitterly cold winter day and wished you could stay in bed? Well, some animals take this to the extreme and miss out winter completely. They avoid the cold and lack of food supplies by going into an inactive state. This is called hibernation, which is a bit like sleeping but with their body functions turned down, or off, to save energy.

Who Hibernates?

A wide range of creatures hibernate, including mammals (such as opossums, skunks, bats and some bears), snails, tortoises and even some insects. Most birds either tough it out or migrate by flying to warmer climates. However, one bird in the USA, the common poorwill, does hibernate.

COMMON POORWILLS HIBERNATE UNDER SHALLOW ROCKS OR ROTTEN LOGS FOR UP TO FIVE MONTHS.

A WOODCHUCK'S HEART RATE DROPS FROM 80 TO FOUR BEATS PER MINUTE WHEN IT HIBERNATES. ITS TEMPERATURE ALSO PLUMMETS BY MORE THAN 30°C. BRRRR!

Heart of the Matter

During hibernation, a creature shuts down some of its body's functions, or slows them down, so it uses less energy. Breathing and heart rate usually drop and their body temperature may fall too.

A hedgehog's heart rate when it's trotting around might be 190 or 200 beats per minute (bpm), but when it's hibernating it may go down to just 20 bpm.

Weight Gain

Hibernating creatures still use some energy whilst dormant, so most munch their way through as much as they can beforehand to build up their bodies' stores of fat. They gradually use up this fat throughout the period they lie dormant.

The American black bear begins serious noshing in the summer, eating nuts, berries and sometimes honey or small mammals. When the bear hibernates, it can go for 100 days without eating, drinking or going to the toilet.

Bathroom Break

Some hibernating creatures, including certain dormice, raccoons and gophers, wake up during the winter and take a bathroom break, as well as eating food they have stored.

MANY CREATURES HIBERNATE ALONE, BUT GARTER SNAKES IN CANADA HIBERNATE IN LARGE GROUPS FOR WARMTH.

Time to Get Up

Some creatures use the weather or the length of sunlight in a day to decide when to start hibernating. Once in hibernation, chemical systems inside their bodies look after the creatures and may trigger their wake-up calls when spring comes and the temperatures rise.

Summer Slowdown

Hibernation helps many creatures to survive harsh, cold winters, but what about sizzling summers? In some parts of the world these can be just as hostile, with temperatures off the scale and a lack of food and water. Well, some clever critters perform their own summer shutdown in regions with long, dry seasons. This is called aestivation.

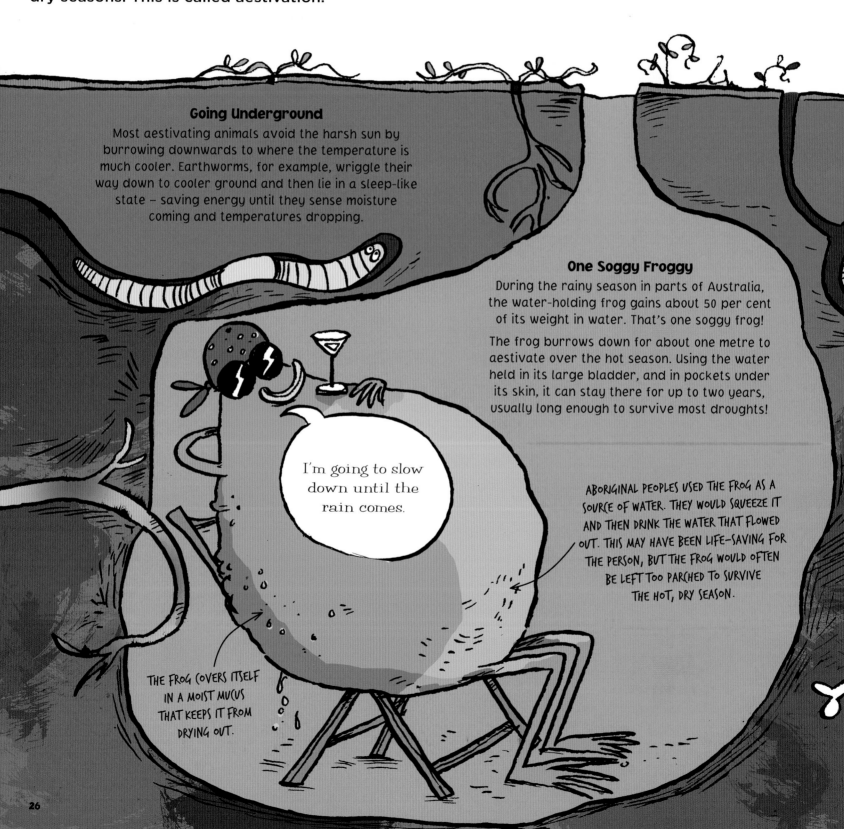

Going Underground

Most aestivating animals avoid the harsh sun by burrowing downwards to where the temperature is much cooler. Earthworms, for example, wriggle their way down to cooler ground and then lie in a sleep-like state – saving energy until they sense moisture coming and temperatures dropping.

One Soggy Froggy

During the rainy season in parts of Australia, the water-holding frog gains about 50 per cent of its weight in water. That's one soggy frog!

The frog burrows down for about one metre to aestivate over the hot season. Using the water held in its large bladder, and in pockets under its skin, it can stay there for up to two years, usually long enough to survive most droughts!

I'm going to slow down until the rain comes.

ABORIGINAL PEOPLES USED THE FROG AS A SOURCE OF WATER. THEY WOULD SQUEEZE IT AND THEN DRINK THE WATER THAT FLOWED OUT. THIS MAY HAVE BEEN LIFE-SAVING FOR THE PERSON, BUT THE FROG WOULD OFTEN BE LEFT TOO PARCHED TO SURVIVE THE HOT, DRY SEASON.

THE FROG COVERS ITSELF IN A MOIST MUCUS THAT KEEPS IT FROM DRYING OUT.

SOME CREATURES, SUCH AS MARPESIA BUTTERFLIES IN SOUTH AMERICA, STAY ABOVE GROUND WHEN THEY AESTIVATE. THESE BUTTERFLIES AESTIVATE BETWEEN JULY AND OCTOBER – HANGING OUT TOGETHER ON BRANCHES IN CLUSTERS OF 50 OR MORE.

Dried Out, Not Died Out

Most fish have gills that draw in oxygen from the water around them. Lungfish, however, have lungs, so they can breathe in oxygen from the air when out of the water.

In the dry season, the freshwater areas they live in shrivel up. But before the water disappears, the fish burrow into the muddy bottom and cover their bodies in mucus. The mucus dries to form a sack that holds moisture inside as the lungfish chill out – dropping their heart rate and slowing their breathing – to stay alive.

AS SOON AS THE RAINS COME THE LUNGFISH IS ABLE TO DETECT THE WATER AND WILL SWIM AWAY FROM ITS BURROW.

LUNGFISH ARE CHAMPION AESTIVATORS – SOME HAVE SURVIVED WITHOUT WATER FOR THREE YEARS!

DIFFERENT SPECIES OF LUNGFISH ARE FOUND IN RIVERS, SWAMPS, PONDS AND LAKES IN AFRICA, AUSTRALIA AND SOUTH AMERICA.

Shut Down, Frozen Out

Some extraordinary creatures can put their lives on hold. This is called cryptobiosis and it sees them suspend most, or all of, their biological systems in response to extreme cold or dry conditions. Some nematodes, a primitive type of microscopic worm, can shut down in dry conditions for years at a time. Other creatures can survive cripplingly cold winters by letting parts of their bodies freeze.

I can't wait for spring!

Deep-freeze Frog

If an animal freezes, the water in its body usually forms expanding ice crystals that can damage its insides and cause it to die. However, the wood frog *Rana sylvatica* is special, it can survive cold winters by using glucose in its body as an antifreeze.

1. SKIN FREEZES FIRST, TURNING THE WOOD FROG HARD AND CRISPY!

2. WATER IN THE FROG'S BLOOD FREEZES – DUE TO SPECIAL PROTEINS IN ITS BLOOD. THIS SUCKS WATER OUT OF THE FROG'S CELLS.

3. THE FROG'S HEART AND KIDNEYS STOP WORKING, BUT IT STAYS ALIVE AND COMES ROUND WHEN THE WEATHER WARMS UP.

4. THE FROG'S LIVER MAKES LOTS OF SUGARY GLUCOSE THAT FLOWS INTO THE FROG'S CELLS – IT WORKS LIKE ANTIFREEZE IN A CAR ENGINE AND STOPS ICE DAMAGE TO CELLS.

5. WHEN WARMER WEATHER COMES, THE FROG THAWS. WATER FLOWS BACK INTO THE CELLS, ITS HEART RESTARTS AND THE FROG STARTS TO BREATHE. IT'S BACK!

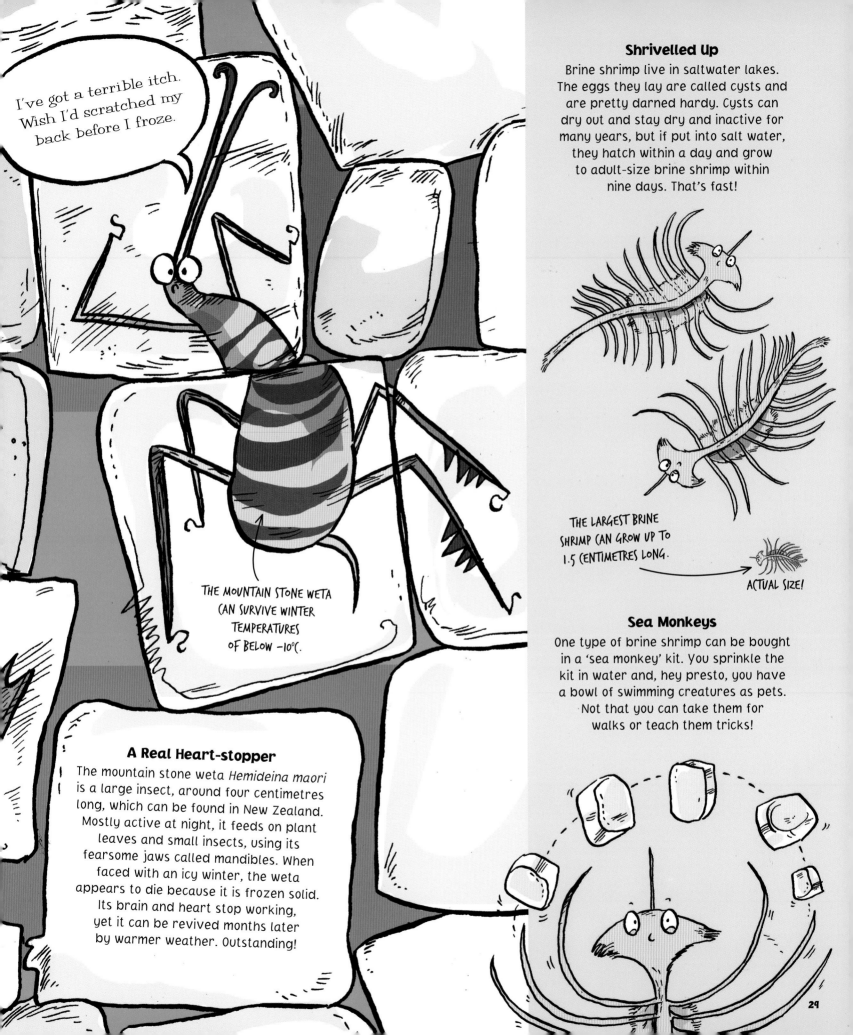

I've got a terrible itch. Wish I'd scratched my back before I froze.

THE MOUNTAIN STONE WETA CAN SURVIVE WINTER TEMPERATURES OF BELOW –10°C.

A Real Heart-stopper

The mountain stone weta *Hemideina maori* is a large insect, around four centimetres long, which can be found in New Zealand. Mostly active at night, it feeds on plant leaves and small insects, using its fearsome jaws called mandibles. When faced with an icy winter, the weta appears to die because it is frozen solid. Its brain and heart stop working, yet it can be revived months later by warmer weather. Outstanding!

Shrivelled Up

Brine shrimp live in saltwater lakes. The eggs they lay are called cysts and are pretty darned hardy. Cysts can dry out and stay dry and inactive for many years, but if put into salt water, they hatch within a day and grow to adult-size brine shrimp within nine days. That's fast!

THE LARGEST BRINE SHRIMP CAN GROW UP TO 1.5 CENTIMETRES LONG.

ACTUAL SIZE!

Sea Monkeys

One type of brine shrimp can be bought in a 'sea monkey' kit. You sprinkle the kit in water and, hey presto, you have a bowl of swimming creatures as pets. Not that you can take them for walks or teach them tricks!

29

Ultimate Survivors

Lungfish and brine shrimp are pretty tough, but they're not as hardy as tardigrades. Nothing is! Also known as water bears, these death-defying critters are short, plump and have eight stubby legs with tiny hooks on their feet. There are more than 400 different species of these creatures, ranging in size from 0.1 to 1.6 millimetres long.

All-weather Water Bears

Tardigrades can be found across much of planet Earth. Most species prefer moist environments, such as sediment at the bottom of a river, but some have been found on chilly mountains, on baking hot beaches and in bubbling hot springs.

ONE LITRE OF WATER AND MUD IN A SEA ESTUARY CAN CONTAIN AS MANY AS 25,000 TARDIGRADES!

TARDIGRADES SLURP THE JUICES OUT OF THEIR FOOD, WHICH CAN INCLUDE OTHER TARDIGRADES! YES, SOME SPECIES ARE CANNIBALS! MOST PREFER THE SAP FROM PLANTS, THOUGH.

150°C

Hot Stuff!

Scientists have really given tardigrades a battering in experiments. Some have been heated to temperatures above 150°C or cooled to -100°C. Yet they manage to tough it out and pull through afterwards.

All Dried Out

Unlike other living things, tardigrades can survive for a long time without water. Tardigrades are normally made up of about 85 per cent water (you are about 70 per cent water). But in really dry conditions, their bodies can dry out to less than three per cent water. They can stay that way for TEN YEARS. Incredible!

A REAL TARDIGRADE
(AS SEEN UNDER A MICROSCOPE – MAGNIFIED 250 TIMES)

10 YEAR CALENDAR

A DRIED-OUT TARDIGRADE IS CALLED A TUN AND IS SO LIGHT THAT WINDS CAN PICK IT UP AND CARRY IT FOR HUNDREDS OF KILOMETRES.

Tardi-nauts!

In 2007, tardigrades went on a mission into space. High above the Earth's surface, the troop were sent outside their spacecraft, the Foton M3. However, they weren't given spacesuits, so they had to survive without air, water or protection from the Sun's harmful ultraviolet (UV) rays. Astonishingly, many of them survived and came back to Earth alive!

I SURVIVED SPACE!

31

Double Trouble

Nothing lives for ever, but copies of some creatures can be made. Cloning is the creation of a living thing that is an exact genetic copy of another living thing. It is very complicated and tricky to do, but it involves copying the special code inside the cells of a living thing, which is called, deep breath, . . . *de-oxy-ribo-nucleic acid*. Phew! Luckily, scientists call it DNA for short.

RALPH WAS THE FIRST RAT TO BE CLONED. HE WAS BORN IN 2003 AFTER LOTS OF WORK BY CHINESE AND FRENCH SCIENTISTS.

SIX YEARS EARLIER IN A LABORATORY IN HAWAII, CUMULINA HAD BECOME THE FIRST CLONED MOUSE.

Hey, Hey, it's DNA

Living things usually get half their DNA from their mother and half from their father. As a result, a new living thing is formed that is different to the parents. Cloning is different, because it involves making an exact copy of the DNA of just ONE living thing.

Feeling Sheepish

On the 5 July 1996, a sheep called Dolly was born. Big deal – thousands of other sheep were also born on that day. But Dolly was different because she didn't have a father! She was a genetic copy of her mother; biologically identical in every single way and the first large mammal to be cloned.

Dolly started life in a test tube. DNA was taken from her mother's cells and placed inside an egg taken from another sheep. This was then put inside a different mother sheep to grow and develop to become Dolly.

Copy Cat

When Nicky the cat died in 2003, her owner Julie was heartbroken, so she paid around £35,000 to a company that cloned animals.

In 2004, Julie got a new kitten that she named Little Nicky, who had been cloned from Nicky's DNA – the first cloned pet cat. Little Nicky looked just like the original and Julie was delighted.

Puppy Facts

Scientists in South Korea were the first to produce a cloned dog: an Afghan hound named Snuppy, who was born in 2005.

In 2009, a group of six cloned golden Labradors in South Korea began work as sniffer dogs, sniffing out suspicious baggage at an airport. They had all been cloned from a single dog and were all given the same name – Toppy!

CLONING IS FAR FROM EASY. SCIENTISTS HAD 276 FAILED ATTEMPTS BEFORE THEY CREATED DOLLY!

Future Undead

Did you know that 99 per cent of all species that have lived on Earth have already died out? Once a species has become well and truly extinct, there's no way back. Well, there hasn't been yet, but that may change. Scientists are working on ways to use cloning techniques to try to bring extinct species back from the dead.

Mammoth Task

Mammoths mostly died out about 10,000 years ago, although small populations on isolated islands may have lasted until 4,000 years ago. Some mammoth bodies have been found frozen in the Arctic tundra. Scientists hope that the DNA in one of these bodies may one day allow them to clone this woolly relative of the elephant.

Living Proof

Cloning takes bags of patience and lots of hard work, but it also needs cells from which to extract some of the extinct creature's DNA. After a creature dies, cells begin to break down and the DNA inside them starts to be lost. After about 500 years, there's only half the DNA in a cell that there was at the outset. This makes it far harder to potentially clone something that is truly ancient.

AN ENTIRE ADULT MAMMOTH WAS FOUND PRESERVED IN A BLOCK OF ICE IN SIBERIA, RUSSIA

THE 23 TONNE BLOCK OF ICE WAS AIRLIFTED BY THE WORLD'S LARGEST HELICOPTER TO A LABORATORY IN RUSSIA.

Ibex Test

The Pyrenean ibex was a type of mountain goat that used to live in mountains in northern Spain and southern France. In 2000, the last one died. Shortly before, scientists took samples of its skin and stored them. Nine years later, a cloned Pyrenean ibex was born.

THE CLONED PYRENEAN IBEX ONLY SURVIVED A SHORT TIME BUT IT WAS THE FIRST EXTINCT SPECIES BROUGHT BACK TO LIFE.

Thylacine

Carolina parakeet

Pyrenean ibex

SCIENTISTS ARE WORKING ON PIECING TOGETHER THE DNA OF SEVERAL EXTINCT SPECIES, SUCH AS THE CAROLINA PARAKEET AND THE THYLACINE, WITH THE HOPE OF BRINGING THEM BACK FROM THE DEAD IN THE FUTURE.

COMING SOON
T-REX

Jurassic Lark

Relax, you won't be ravaged by a raptor or terrorized by a T-Rex anytime soon. Nothing even close to a complete strand of dinosaur DNA has survived the 65-million-year stretch since the last dinosaurs were alive.

Deadly Prisoners

Death is never nice but some deaths in the natural world seem worse than others. Imagine being swallowed whole and gradually digested, or poisoned by an exploding termite. What terrible ways to go! It's not easy to survive in the animal world – especially with this lot around . . .

BLACK WIDOW SPIDER
PRISONER 89-29-723

TERMITE
PRISONER 78-40-307

THE FEMALE BLACK WIDOW SPIDER ISN'T THE ONLY ONE TO SNACK ON ITS MATE. FEMALES OF THE EUROPEAN GARDEN SPIDER *ARANAEUS DIADEMATUS*, THE COMMON PRAYING MANTIS *MANTIS RELIGIOSA* AND SOME SPECIES OF SCORPIONS ALSO DO THIS!

Love and Death
You may have heard of human couples having arguments, but the female black widow spider takes it to the limit. Straight after breeding with her male mate, the female will sometimes gobble him up!

Kamikaze Creatures
Termite nest invaders need to keep an eye out for worker termites *Neocapritermes taracua*. They have tiny blue pouches on their backs that contain a powerful poison. When their nest is threatened, the worker termite explodes, scattering the poison to kill the attackers.

You'll never get me now!

Light Up My Life

Some creatures carry their own light source with them inside their bodies. This is created by chemicals mixing together in a reaction that gives off light. Scientists call this bioluminescence and it can be a useful tool in the fight for survival.

Cookiecutter sharks and anglerfish emit light as a way to attract prey. Whereas dinoflagellates give off light to sacrifice themselves in order to help other dinoflagellates survive.

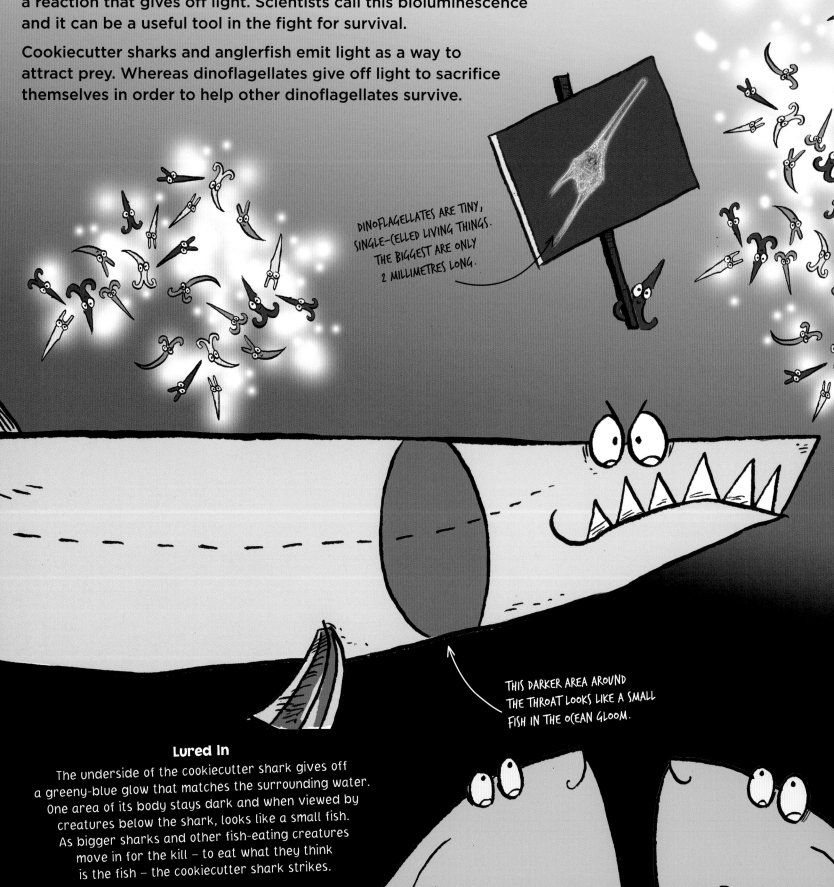

DINOFLAGELLATES ARE TINY, SINGLE-CELLED LIVING THINGS. THE BIGGEST ARE ONLY 2 MILLIMETRES LONG.

THIS DARKER AREA AROUND THE THROAT LOOKS LIKE A SMALL FISH IN THE OCEAN GLOOM.

Lured In

The underside of the cookiecutter shark gives off a greeny-blue glow that matches the surrounding water. One area of its body stays dark and when viewed by creatures below the shark, looks like a small fish. As bigger sharks and other fish-eating creatures move in for the kill – to eat what they think is the fish – the cookiecutter shark strikes.

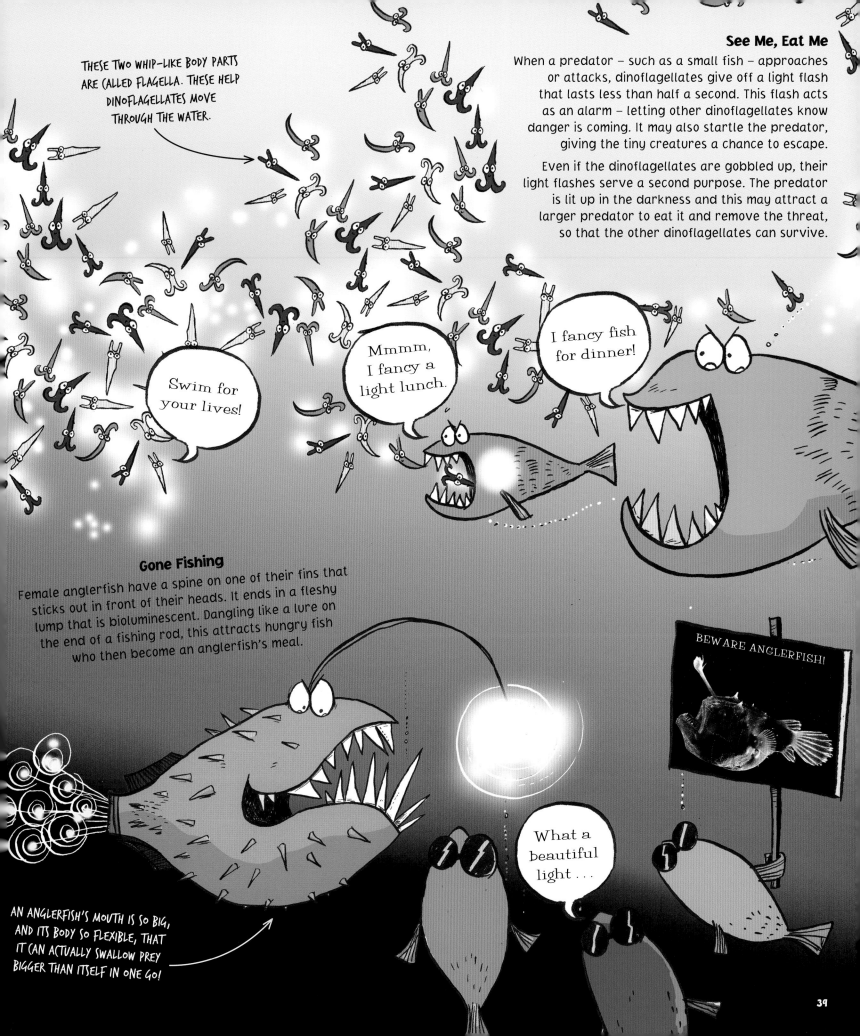

THESE TWO WHIP-LIKE BODY PARTS ARE CALLED FLAGELLA. THESE HELP DINOFLAGELLATES MOVE THROUGH THE WATER.

See Me, Eat Me

When a predator – such as a small fish – approaches or attacks, dinoflagellates give off a light flash that lasts less than half a second. This flash acts as an alarm – letting other dinoflagellates know danger is coming. It may also startle the predator, giving the tiny creatures a chance to escape.

Even if the dinoflagellates are gobbled up, their light flashes serve a second purpose. The predator is lit up in the darkness and this may attract a larger predator to eat it and remove the threat, so that the other dinoflagellates can survive.

Swim for your lives!

Mmmm, I fancy a light lunch.

I fancy fish for dinner!

Gone Fishing

Female anglerfish have a spine on one of their fins that sticks out in front of their heads. It ends in a fleshy lump that is bioluminescent. Dangling like a lure on the end of a fishing rod, this attracts hungry fish who then become an anglerfish's meal.

BEWARE ANGLERFISH!

What a beautiful light . . .

AN ANGLERFISH'S MOUTH IS SO BIG, AND ITS BODY SO FLEXIBLE, THAT IT CAN ACTUALLY SWALLOW PREY BIGGER THAN ITSELF IN ONE GO!

39

Some creatures lose the will to live, think or do almost anything for themselves when they are taken over by another living thing. They pretty much become . . .

ZOMBIES!

WHO'S THE BOSS?

If you're a crab, watch out for *Sacculina carcini* – it's a real bossy boots! This orange barnacle drifts in the sea until it spots a crab and climbs inside its shell. The barnacle then grows fine strands, called tendrils, throughout the crab's body so it can steal nutrients from the crab's blood to feed itself. Naughty!

But there's far worse to come. These tendrils grow into the crab's brain . . . and control it. Seriously! The crab no longer looks for a mate or moults its shell. All it does is what the bossy barnacle tells it to do!

BARNACLE HEADQUARTERS

Doctor Barnacle

Move left, crab. Now lift your claw . . . I love being in control. Mwahahahaha!

Barnacle Babysitter
When the barnacle makes babies, the zombie crab will even look after them as if they were their own.

HERE LIES A POOR SPIDER

Certain wasps inject their larvae (young) into a spider's body, along with a cocktail of chemicals that causes the spider to lose its mind. Instead of spinning webs as spiders normally do, the zombie spider spins a cocoon round itself.

It's the last bit of work the zombie spider does, as it then dies and is eaten by the wasp larvae, which use the cocoon as a place to safely turn into young wasps.

A LOUSE-Y WAY TO GO

To avoid getting eaten by birds, woodlice hide under pieces of wood. However, if tiny parasites (spiny-headed worms) get inside a woodlouse and release chemicals to take over its brain, this can cause the woodlouse to put itself in danger. The zombie woodlouse will leave the safety of its shelter and venture out into the open, where it will soon be snapped up by a bird.

Spiny-headed worms need the woodlouse to be eaten so that they can continue with their life cycle.

Dead Certain

Dead certain that you now know all about the amazing creatures in this book?

Well, take this tough test of your knowledge and see how you do.
If you get more than 10 out of 15 right (without peeking at the previous pages or the answers below) then you've done really, really well!

1. What sort of creature do orange barnacles take over the mind of?

2. Was Snuppy, Dolly or Tuppy the name given to the first successfully cloned dog?

3. Can tardigrades survive being dried out for six months, eighteen months or ten years?

4. What type of creature were the runaways nicknamed the Tamworth Two?

5. Which brave pigeon carried a vital message that saved almost 200 US soldiers during World War I?

6. Does a Livingstone's cichlid, a hognose snake or a lungfish play dead to attract its prey?

7. What type of puppy survived being flushed down the toilet: an Afghan hound, a cocker spaniel, a poodle or a Labrador?

8. How long do most adult mayflies live for: one day, one month or one year?

9. In which country in the world would you find the rare bird, the takahé?

10. How many floors above ground did Sugar the cat fall from and survive: 11 floors, 16 floors or 19 floors?

11. Was a live mammoth, Pyrenean ibex or thylacine born after cloning by scientists in 2009?

Extra Hard Questions:

12. How long does it take for a Venus flytrap's leaves to close around an insect to trap it?

13. Which creature's heart rate drops from 190-200 beats per minute to just 20 beats per minute when it hibernates?

14. What do lungfish and Marpesia butterflies have in common?

15. What was the name of the spacecraft that carried tardigrades into space in 2007?

Answers:
1. Crabs 2. Snuppy 3. Ten years 4. Pigs 5. Cher Ami 6. Livingstone's cichlid 7. Cocker spaniel 8. One day 9. New Zealand 10. 19 floors 11. Pyrenean ibex 12. Half a second 13. Hedgehog 14. They both destivate 15. Foton M3

Brilliant Books

Here are some other good books to help you learn more about the different topics in this book.

- *Cloning and Genetic Engineering*
  Nicola Barber, Franklin Watts, 2013

  Learn both sides of the story of the debate about whether we should clone animals.

- *Countdown to Extinction: Animals in Danger!*
  David Burnie, OUP, 2008

  A guide to the threats many creatures face to their survival.

- *Extreme Science: Extreme Lunch!*
  Ross Piper, A&C Black, 2009

  An exciting, easy-to-read book on some of the most outrageous ways animals kill and eat their prey.

- *National Geographic Kids: 125 True Stories of Amazing Animals*
  National Geographic Society, 2012

  Tales of incredible animals, including heroic pets.

Wonderful Weblinks

Want to see some of the creatures in this book in action or learn more about them?

Then head to the internet and check out these useful weblinks.

- Learn more about the hognose snake:
  www.thehognosesnake.co.uk

- See a rare Lord Howe's stick insect crawl across the presenter's hand and learn about scientific efforts to increase their numbers:
  www.youtube.com/watch?v=ITmtMpiV430

- Listen to the Galapagos tortoise and learn more about these amazing creatures:
  http://animals.nationalgeographic.co.uk/animals/reptiles/galapagos-tortoise

- Read and see more about mayflies at the entertaining Buglife website:
  www.buglife.org.uk/bugs-and-habitats/mayfly

Glossary

Abattoir
A place where animals that are reared for their meat are killed.

Aestivate
When a creature goes into a dormant state because of hot and dry conditions.

Bioluminescence
Light given off by a living thing, such as a firefly or certain type of fish.

Breeding
The process by which creatures reproduce to create offspring.

Carbon dating
A scientific technique to estimate the age of a once-living thing.

Darwin, Charles
A famous scientist who sailed to the Galapagos Islands off the coast of South America and developed important theories about how animals evolve.

Digestive juices
The juices inside the digestive system of a creature, which break food down into substances that the body can absorb.

Estimate
To make a good guess about something, such as the numbers of a living thing.

Estuary
A place where a river meets and flows into a sea.

Extinction
When a species of living thing completely dies out so that there are none of them left alive.

Glucose
A type of sugar that provides energy for living things.

Hibernate
When a creature goes into a dormant state because of cold conditions.

Hurricane
A powerful type of tropical storm with winds that speed round in a circle at over 120 kilometres per hour.

Insects
Small creatures with six legs and bodies formed of three parts: the head, middle section (called a thorax) and the abdomen.

Laboratory

A place where scientists work and perform experiments and research.

Life cycle

The major steps in the life of a creature from its birth to how it grows, breeds and dies.

Mammals

A type of animal, such as mice, cows and humans. They have a backbone, are warm-blooded, usually give birth to live young and feed their young on milk.

Microscope

A scientific instrument that magnifies (makes bigger) very small things so that people can view them.

Migrate

To move from one area to another at different times of the year.

Moult

To shed a layer of fur, skin or an outer skeleton.

Nutrients

Substances that provide energy and materials to allow a living thing to grow or repair itself.

Nymphs

The young stage in the life of many insects before they become fully-grown adults.

Oxygen

A gas found in air and water that almost all creatures need in order to stay alive.

Parasites

Plants or creatures that live in, or on, another living thing from which they gain their food.

Poison

A substance that can cause harm or death to the living things that eat it.

Population

The number of one creature, either in total across the world or in a particular place.

Predators

Creatures that hunt and feed on other creatures.

Prey

A creature hunted or caught for food.

Species

A particular type of living thing. Individuals in a species can breed with each other to produce new members of their species.

Tundra

Large, cold regions in, or close to, the Arctic Circle with no trees.

UV (ultraviolet) rays

Ultraviolet light is a type of light that we cannot see. It travels in waves from the Sun and other bodies in space. Strong ultraviolet rays can be harmful to living things.

World War I

A war that began in 1914 and ended in 1918, which involved many countries around the world.

Index

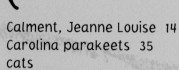